Animal Architects

Daniel Nassar

Julio Antonio Blasco

Laurence King Publishing

LAURENCE KING

Published in 2015 by
Laurence King Publishing Ltd.
361–373 City Road
London EC1V 1LR
T +44 (0)20 7841 6900
F +44 (0)20 7841 6910
email: enquiries@laurenceking.com
www.laurenceking.com

Reprinted 2015

Copyright © Zahorí de Ideas,
Barcelona, Spain
Copyright © Text: Daniel Nassar
Copyright © Illustrations and Design:
Julio Antonio Blasco
Original title: *Animales Arquitectos*

This English edition is published by
arrangement with Zahorí de Ideas,
Barcelona, Spain.

A catalog record for this book
is available from British Library

ISBN: 978 1 78067 654 8

Printed in China

Animal Architects

04. **A mobile residence**

06. **A suspended house**

08. **A made-to-measure home**

10. **An airy spire**

12. **An underground garden**

14. **A river den**

16. **A tadpole pool**

18. **A commuter town**

20. **A foamy refuge**

22. **A suspension bridge**

24. **A room with a view**

26. **A treetop attic**

28. **The lover's gazebo**

30. **A tiny apartment**

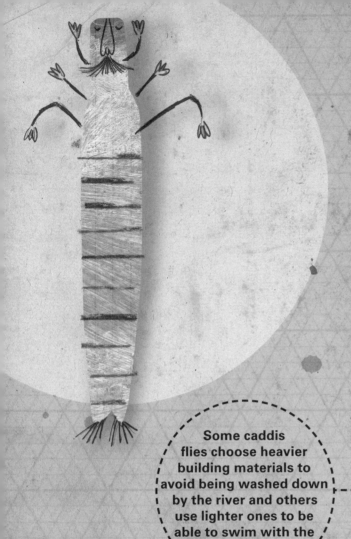

CADDIS FLY

Trichoptera, the Greek name for **caddis fly**, literally means "hairy wings." This insect, closely related to moths, undergoes a complete transformation from the egg to a larva and finally to a pupa. It lives underwater during the larva and pupa stages, and then becomes a flying insect as an adult.

The fishing nets are woven with a small or large mesh, depending on the speed of the river currents and the size of the catch.

Some caddis flies choose heavier building materials to avoid being washed down by the river and others use lighter ones to be able to swim with the house on.

A mobile residence

The larva of the caddis fly builds a mobile house to protect itself until it reaches adulthood. It constructs the house by gluing hard materials such as small stones, sand, dried leaves, and twigs to its larval body using a self-made sticky silk.

How it's built

Good materials: the caddis fly chooses widely available materials from its surroundings and **selects** those tougher than its own shell to build its camouflaged "case."

With windows: the silk is used to **glue** all the materials to the body, **leaving holes** for the head and legs so it can move and eat without leaving the house.

Gone fishing: the silk is also used to **make** fishing nets to catch food from the flowing river.

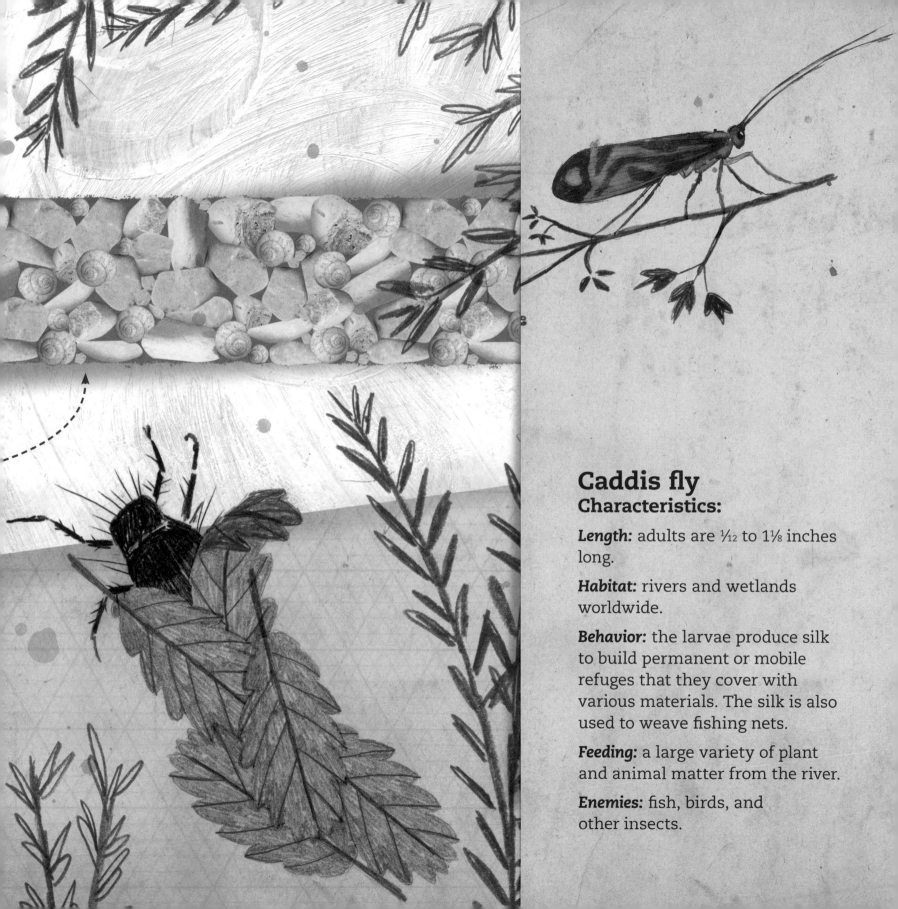

Caddis fly
Characteristics:

Length: adults are $\frac{1}{12}$ to $1\frac{1}{8}$ inches long.

Habitat: rivers and wetlands worldwide.

Behavior: the larvae produce silk to build permanent or mobile refuges that they cover with various materials. The silk is also used to weave fishing nets.

Feeding: a large variety of plant and animal matter from the river.

Enemies: fish, birds, and other insects.

AFRICAN WEAVERBIRD

The African weaverbird belongs to a large family of small **birds** with rounded, conical beaks. Their name comes from their **ability** to **weave** beautiful, perfectly shaped nests. The males of many species are brightly colored with red or yellow and black plumage.

A suspended house

The male weaverbird builds the nest to:

- attract and impress the female with his building techniques;
- incubate and rear the chicks in safety.

Occasionally the weaverbird extends the door downward to form an entry tunnel that provides more protection.

How it's built

A meticulous architect: the male starts by **stripping** shoots and green leaves to form thin and flexible threads. He then **ties** the fine threads to a sturdy branch using his beak and feet, leaving the ends loose. Then, he **weaves** a ring at the end of the loose ends. This ring becomes the nest entrance and will be used as a support while he weaves the rest of the nest.

An interior decorator: the female adds the finishing touches by **decorating** the interior with grass, cotton, and feathers.

A nest village: sometimes weaver birds build their nests close to each other and cover them all by building a shared roof out of straw.

The nest is a labor of love for the male. He makes it as beautiful as possible to impress the female with his construction skills.

Some weaverbird nests have two doorways, so that the birds can enter and leave at the same time.

African weaverbird
Characteristics:

Weight: ⅞ to 1¼ ounces.

Length: 6 to 7 inches.

Wingspan: 6 to 10 inches.

Habitat: most live in Sub-Saharan Africa but a few species live in tropical Asia and Australia. They are found in savannahs—grassy plains dotted with trees.

Behavior: when breeding they pair up, but they like living in groups and are often found near human populations.

Feeding: mainly seeds or insects.

Enemies: snakes and other birds.

MONARCH BUTTERFLY

This butterfly is well known for traveling long distances in groups. These journeys in search of warm weather can cover **thousands of miles**. The monarch, like other butterflies, has a four-stage life cycle: egg, caterpillar, **chrysalis**, and butterfly. The chrysalis is like a house where an amazing **transformation** happens!

Adult monarch butterflies normally live for 4–5 weeks, but when they are migrating they can survive for much longer—up to 7–8 months.

A made-to-measure home

The chrysalis is the refuge where the change from caterpillar to butterfly takes place. This takes 8–13 days, or longer in winter. The chrysalis has a capsule shape and hangs from a branch hidden by leaves. To start with it is green, but then it becomes translucent before the colors of the new butterfly are revealed.

How it's built

Finding the right site: the caterpillar **chooses** a branch from one of the trees that it feeds from and **sticks** to it by its tail, using its own silk.

Under construction: the chrysalis is **formed** around the hanging caterpillar and is made of **chitin**, the same material found in insect shells.

Let's fly away: the caterpillar transforms inside the chrysalis into a butterfly. It finally emerges by **breaking** free from the capsule and **extending** its wings.

The monarch caterpillar is a voracious feeder. After hatching from its egg, it grows 2,000 times bigger, and sheds its skin five times.

Monarch butterfly
Characteristics:

Weight: ¹⁄₁₀₀ to ¹⁄₄₀ of an ounce.

Length: 1½ to 2 inches including the antennae (adults).

Wingspan: 3¾ to 4 inches (adults).

Habitat: migrates between North America and Central and South America, and it is also found in parts of Europe, Asia, and Australasia.

Behavior: every year monarch butterflies make the long journey from Mexico to Canada. Some cross the Atlantic Ocean and reach Europe.

Feeding: mainly feeds on milkweed, a plant with milky sap.

Enemies: some birds and mice that are immune to the venom from the monarch butterfly.

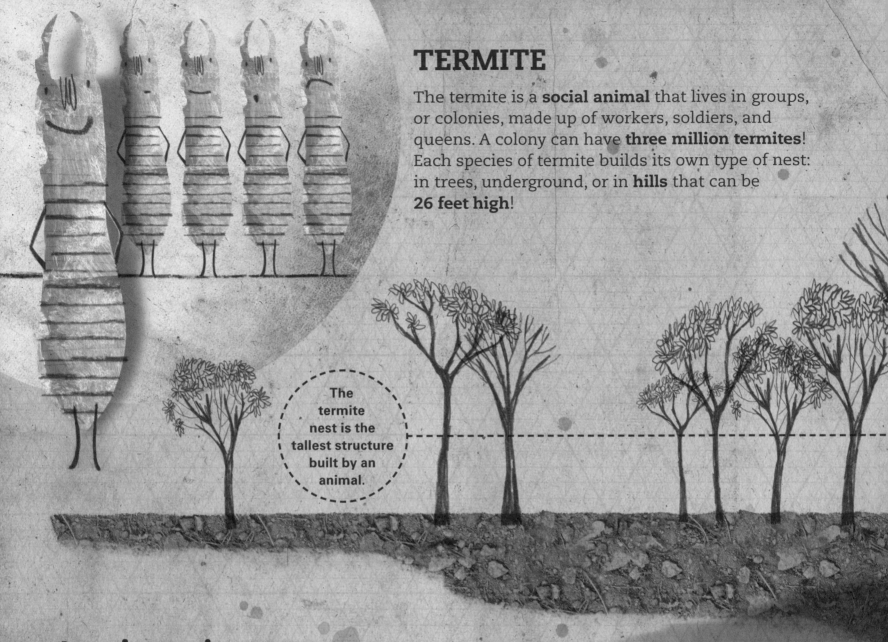

TERMITE

The termite is a **social animal** that lives in groups, or colonies, made up of workers, soldiers, and queens. A colony can have **three million termites**! Each species of termite builds its own type of nest: in trees, underground, or in **hills** that can be **26 feet high**!

The termite nest is the tallest structure built by an animal.

An airy spire

The termite nest is a tall structure that is used as:

- a place to live and organize the colony;
- a place to bring up baby termites;
- protection against bright light and high temperatures.

How it's built

A building site manager: the queen gives orders to the termites. A place is **chosen** close to the trees and bushes the termites feed on.

Teamwork: the worker termites build the nest slowly using mud mixed with soil, saliva, and poo.

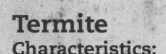

Termite
Characteristics:

Length: ⅙ to ¾ of an inch, depending on the species and type.

Habitat: Africa, South America, and Australia. Recently, termites have also been found in Europe. They tend to live in woods and savannahs.

Behavior: they live in colonies of as many as three million termites. They avoid light except when the queen termites grow wings and go on a flight to search for a partner to create a new colony.

Feeding: cellulose from dead wood that is predigested by the worker termites who then feed the rest of the colony.

Enemies: mainly ants.

Clever engineering: the center of the nest contains the living rooms and many ventilation tunnels are **built** around it to maintain a pleasant temperature. The termites also dig large underground corridors that connect the termite nest to the trees that provide their food.

LEAFCUTTER ANT

The ant is a social insect that lives in colonies organized into social classes. Every class specializes in a particular task: the soldiers protect the group; the workers collect food, build homes, and care for babies; and the queens lay the eggs. Leafcutter ants build fabulous nests with many features, including gardens!

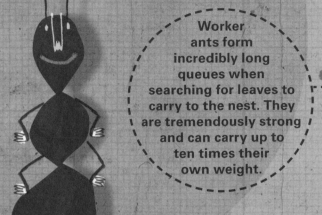

Worker ants form incredibly long queues when searching for leaves to carry to the nest. They are tremendously strong and can carry up to ten times their own weight.

An underground garden

Nests are underground and include gardens, tunnels, and even rooms for the garbage!

The nest serves various purposes:

- to grow the fungus that the ants eat;
- to raise the new members of the colony;
- to achieve the ideal temperature for eggs to develop and hatch.

How it's built

At the Queen's service: the queen looks for a good plot in a clearing in the woods. The ground needs to be firm but easy to excavate.

Diggers in action: the workers responsible for digging start by making numerous tunnels. The soil from the digging site is used to form a small pile full of "chimneys." The tunnels **eventually become** big chambers.

Garden matters: the central chambers are used as fungus gardens and the nurseries to feed and rear the little ones. The smallest ants of the group, known as "nanny gardeners," work in these zones.

Cleaning services: the biggest chambers are located on the edges of the nest, and are used for **collecting** waste. The medium-sized worker ants are in charge there, **managing** the waste.

Fresh air: the chewed leaves end up producing hot gases that go up the central chimneys to the surface. These currents cause fresh air to enter the small chimneys on the sides.

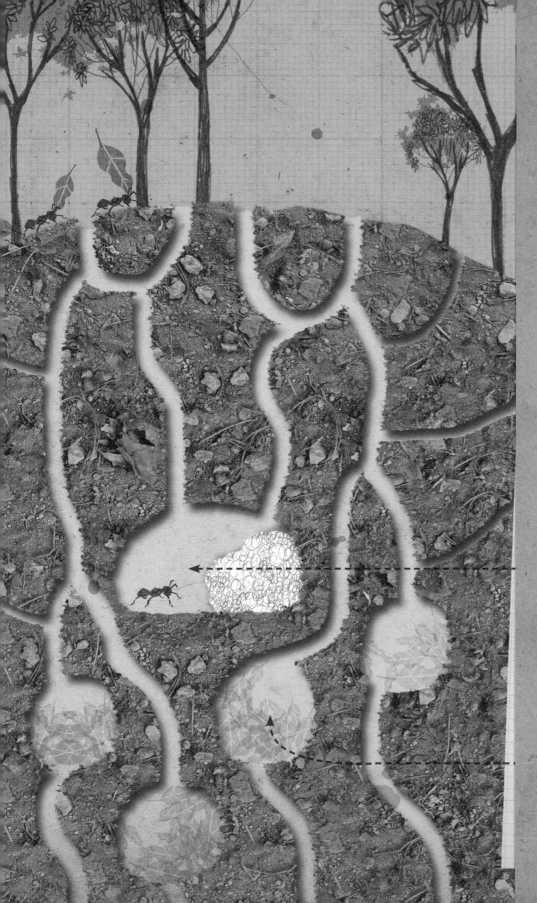

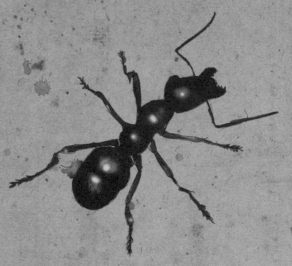

Leafcutter ant
Characteristics:

Length: ¹⁄₁₀ to 1 inch, depending on the species.

Habitat: South and Central American woodlands.

Behavior: they live in highly organized groups with several social classes, and every class can have more than five million individuals. The ants collect leaves that are processed to grow the fungus.

Feeding: a particular type of fungus that grows on the paste made out of chewed leaves, saliva, and excrement.

Enemies: birds, other insects, lizards, and some parasites. Humans from some cultures find them delicious as well!

BEAVER

This skilled **rodent** lives in rivers and streams in woodland areas, where it constructs **dams** and builds its den. Beavers move better in water than on land.

A river den

The beaver constructs the den together with its partner to:

- protect the family from other animals such as bears and wolves;
- shelter during the cold winter;
- store food (branches, bark, and foliage) for when the river freezes.

How it's built

The perfect site: the couple chooses a tranquil river with shallow waters of about three feet in depth. They **cut** tree trunks, branches, and bark with their sharp teeth and use these materials to **build** a dam to create a little lake.

A sound foundation: in the center of the lake they **form** a base of stones and mud, then build up a **pile** of branches and foliage until it emerges above the surface of the water.

A sturdy roof: a dome-shaped top made of branches, dried leaves, and interwoven grass is **covered** with wet mud and moss that **hardens** like a rock when frozen.

Entry doors: located under the water are two doors: one to enter and exit, the other to bring in the food.

The chimneys: they leave a hole in the dome for ventilation. They think of every detail!

The beavers can shelter safely inside the den.

The steeper entrance allows them a quick entry and exit.

The gently sloping entrance allows them to bring wood inside.

Security: lastly the beavers **surround** the little lake with a stinky fence made with mud and castoreum (a foul-smelling substance that they produce). The smell is so strong that nobody gets close except members of the family.

Maintenance: they are always repairing the den and extensions. Beavers are very hard-working!

Beaver
Characteristics:

Weight: 45 to 65 pounds.

Length: 30 to 50 inches. The tail is ⅓ of the total length.

Height: 12 inches.

Habitat: rivers and streams of cold woodland areas in North America and Europe.

Behavior: semi-aquatic animal. Lives with partner and in groups. Almost always works at night.

Feeding: herbivorous (leaves, bark, aquatic plants, and fruits).

Enemies: humans are the beaver's worst enemy, but not the only one. Bears, foxes, and fishers are also a threat to them.

GLADIATOR FROG

The frog's name comes from the fierce way the male defends the nest he has built.

The female lays around 3,000 eggs that take 2–3 days to hatch.

A tadpole pool

This frog constructs small pools in order to:

- make a place for the female to lay her eggs;
- create an enclosed area to stop the tadpoles being washed away by the currents or eaten by predators.

How it's built

The minimum effort: the male constructs a little pool by enclosing an area on the shores of a larger pond with a mud wall. Sometimes he uses a pre-existing dip formed by an animal footprint, saving him a lot of work.

Building site inspection: after the pool is finished the female is invited to inspect it. If she approves, he courts her and, when the time comes, she lays the eggs inside the little pool. The male frog guards the floating eggs and when the tadpoles become frogs they jump out of the pool. Hop, splash!

The female frog is very demanding and checks the nest thoroughly before going in. Half of the time she declines.

Gladiator frog
Characteristics:

Length: 2¾ to 3½ inches.

Habitat: wet lowlands of Costa Rica, Panama, Colombia, and Ecuador.

Behavior: the male constructs a pool with mud to attract the female. He defends the nest from attack in a very aggressive manner.

Feeding: eats mostly seeds and insects.

Enemies: snakes, lizards, birds, small mammals, and other male frogs from the same species.

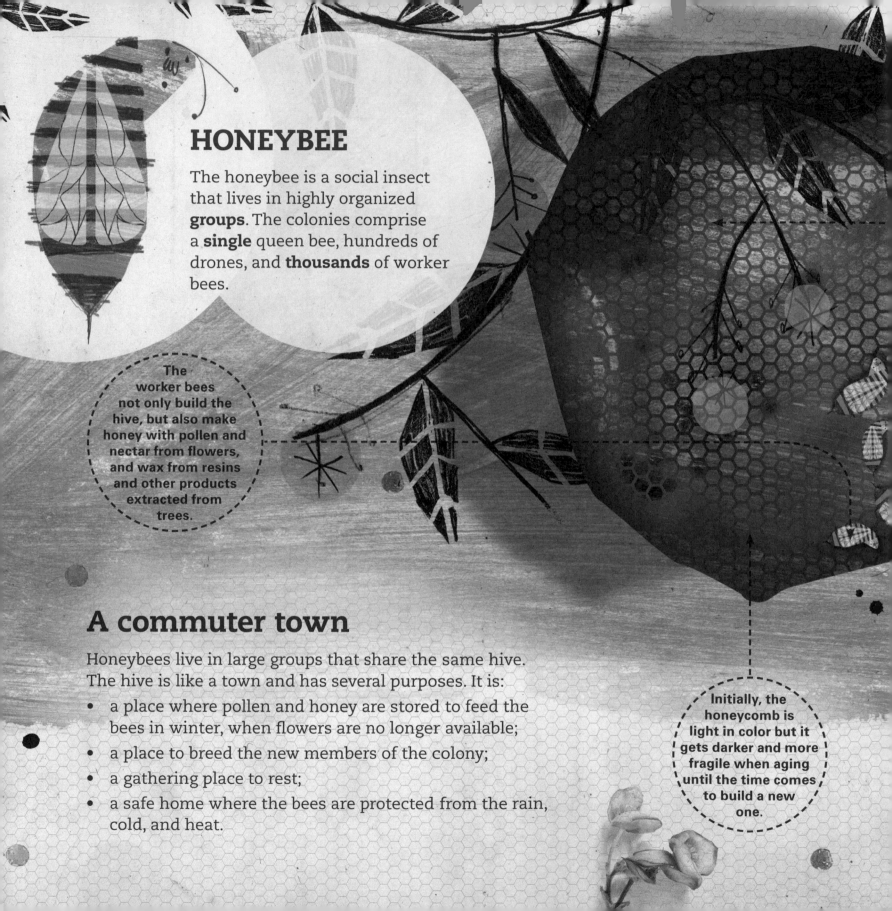

HONEYBEE

The honeybee is a social insect that lives in highly organized **groups**. The colonies comprise a **single** queen bee, hundreds of drones, and **thousands** of worker bees.

The worker bees not only build the hive, but also make honey with pollen and nectar from flowers, and wax from resins and other products extracted from trees.

Initially, the honeycomb is light in color but it gets darker and more fragile when aging until the time comes to build a new one.

A commuter town

Honeybees live in large groups that share the same hive. The hive is like a town and has several purposes. It is:

- a place where pollen and honey are stored to feed the bees in winter, when flowers are no longer available;
- a place to breed the new members of the colony;
- a gathering place to rest;
- a safe home where the bees are protected from the rain, cold, and heat.

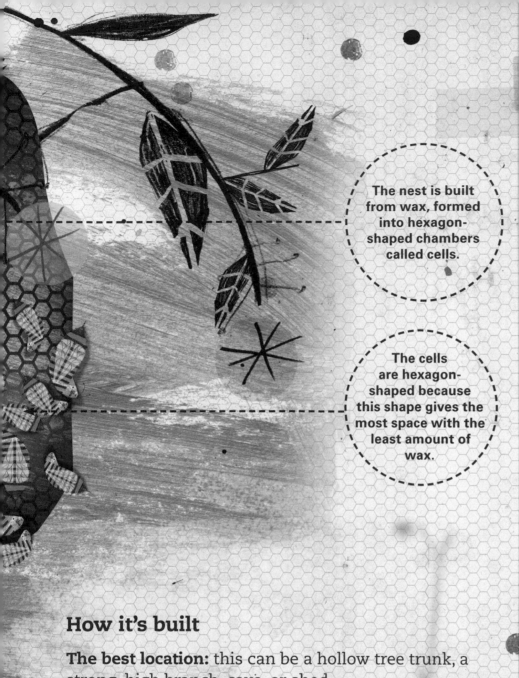

The nest is built from wax, formed into hexagon-shaped chambers called cells.

The cells are hexagon-shaped because this shape gives the most space with the least amount of wax.

How it's built

The best location: this can be a hollow tree trunk, a strong, high branch, cave, or shed.

Buzzing to work: the worker bees clean the surface where the hive will be attached. Unlike a human house, the construction takes place from top to bottom.

Keeping clean: the cells where honey is stored and eggs are laid are covered with wax and propolis (resin paste) to protect them from mold and bacteria.

Honeybee
Characteristics:

Length: worker bees are ½ an inch, the queen is ¾ of an inch, and drones are ⅝ of an inch.

Lifespan: worker bees live for a few weeks but the queen bee can live up to five years.

Habitat: gardens, fields, woods, and clearings worldwide.

Behavior: social animals that live in groups or colonies.

Feeding: herbivorous (pollen, nectar and honey).

Enemies: hornets, mammals (bears, mice, and skunks), and birds (swallows, magpies, and others).

AFRICAN TREE FROG

This frog lives in **trees** and builds its nest on branches overhanging water, using **foam** wrapped in leaves. The nest is a **soft** place to house the eggs and when they hatch, the tadpoles fall straight into the water. Splash! In the water they become frogs.

A foamy refuge

The eggs are fragile, so the frog makes a foamy nest designed to safeguard them.

How it's built

First, the female frog chooses a branch. It must be nice and strong, and over the water.

Ingredients: saliva (spit) produced by the female.

How she does it: she whips the saliva with her legs until a foamy mixture is formed, and lays the eggs inside. The heat hardens the outer layer of the foam but the interior remains soft. The tadpoles grow inside and then dissolve the foam, falling from the cozy nest into the water.

The African tree frog has large front and back legs. Webbing between the frog's toes puffs up with air like a parachute, holding the frog upward as it jumps from tree to tree.

Predators cannot reach the eggs in the nest, as they are laid high up on the tree.

AFRICAN TREE FROG
Characteristics:

Length: 1 to 1¾ inches.

Habitat: near lakes and ponds in tropical wetlands of central Africa.

Feeding: eats a large variety of insect and plant material.

Enemies: they have many enemies including snakes, chameleons, birds, and large fish.

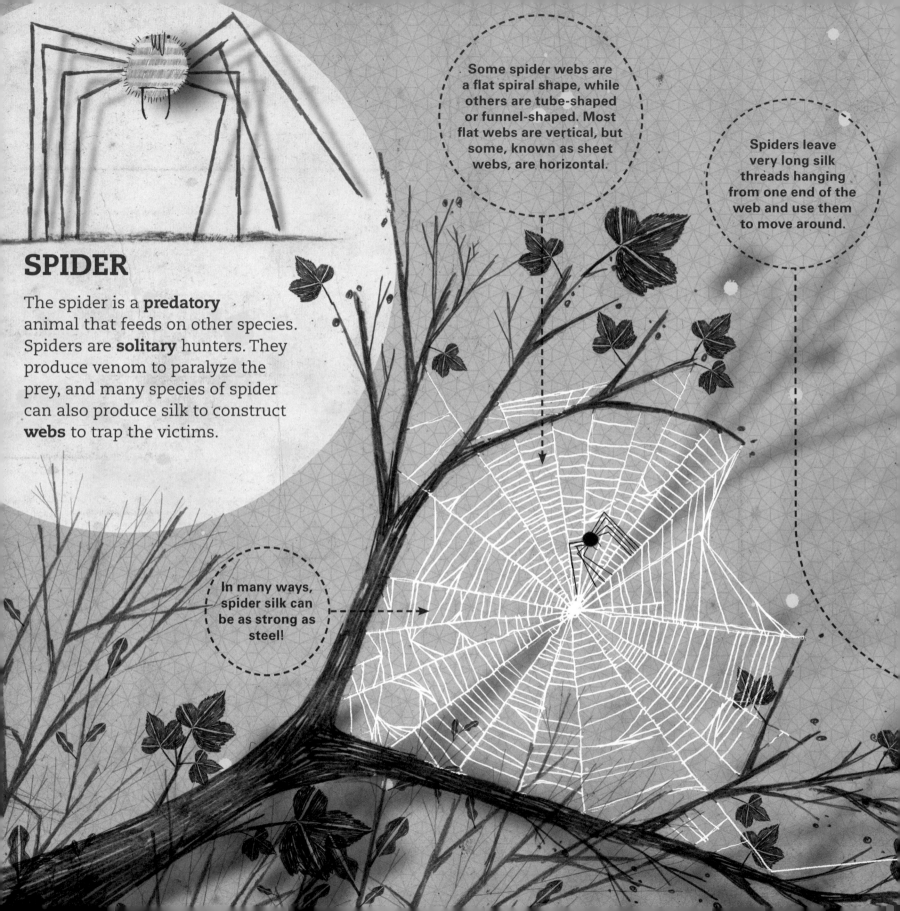

SPIDER

The spider is a **predatory** animal that feeds on other species. Spiders are **solitary** hunters. They produce venom to paralyze the prey, and many species of spider can also produce silk to construct **webs** to trap the victims.

Some spider webs are a flat spiral shape, while others are tube-shaped or funnel-shaped. Most flat webs are vertical, but some, known as sheet webs, are horizontal.

Spiders leave very long silk threads hanging from one end of the web and use them to move around.

In many ways, spider silk can be as strong as steel!

A suspension bridge

The spider **builds** its web for two main reasons:

- to catch flying insects that get accidentally stuck in the web when zooming along;
- to move around safely, far from predators on the ground.

How it's built

A good base: the spider **looks for** a solid support such as branches, stones, or stone crevices on which to attach the silk threads.

Silk for everything: the silk is then **produced** in an organ (gland) in the spider's body. Some spiders can have up to seven glands, each one producing a different type of silk, depending on the use.

The strongest silk is **used** for the threads that stretch across the web and keep it taut. The more flexible and sticky silk is used to **create** a spiral net that attaches to the tightening threads.

Spider

Characteristics:

Length: $\frac{1}{50}$ to 3½ inches.

Habitat: found worldwide in all climate types, from very wet areas to dry lands. Antarctica is the only spider-free continent.

Behavior: lives alone catching each prey one by one with a web. The female tends to be much larger than the male and sometimes she kills and eats the male after mating.

Feeding: eats flying insects that are trapped in the web. The spider paralyzes the victims with venom and then injects digestive juices into them, turning their insides into mush that can be easily eaten.

Enemies: birds, lizards, frogs, fish, and other spiders.

WHITE STORK

The white stork is a very large **migratory** bird that rears its chicks in Europe during spring and summer, and then returns to Africa in winter to escape the cold weather. Storks often build large nests high up on very tall buildings close to human dwellings, and are viewed as good omens.

The white stork feeds water to the chicks by squeezing wet moss directly into their open beaks.

There are many legends about white storks. The best-known myth is the story of the white stork as the bringer of babies. The stork is often shown carrying a "bundle of joy" to new parents.

Nests can grow and become very heavy (the weight of a lion, or 550 lbs!), and sometimes they fall or bring down the structure they are attached to.

How it's built

On top of the world: the male **looks for** a good location somwhere high up, and **starts** the building alone. The female **joins in** once the nest has taken shape.

Deep and secure: the base is built with large branches and fixed to the chosen surface. Then, smaller branches and dried leaves are added along with soil and mud to erect high walls that stop the eggs from falling out.

Very comfy: finally, small leaves and moss are **used** as fillers for maximum comfort. Storks also **make use** of human materials such as clothes, paper, and plastics. Every year, the nest is reused after improvements and extensions are added to it.

A room with a view

The white stork builds its nest to incubate and feed its eggs and chicks. Like most bird nests, it is cup-shaped. The stork builds a very large nest and usually chooses tall human structures for its location.

WHITE STORK
Characteristics:

Weight: 5 to 10 pounds when adult.

Length: 40 to 45 inches.

Wingspan: 60 to 85 inches.

Habitat: prairies, farmland, and shallow wetlands mainly in Europe. In winter, the stork migrates to Sub-Saharan Africa.

Feeding: eats frogs, small rodents, and insects.

Enemies: no known predators. Humans and the destruction of the stork's habitat are their main threats.

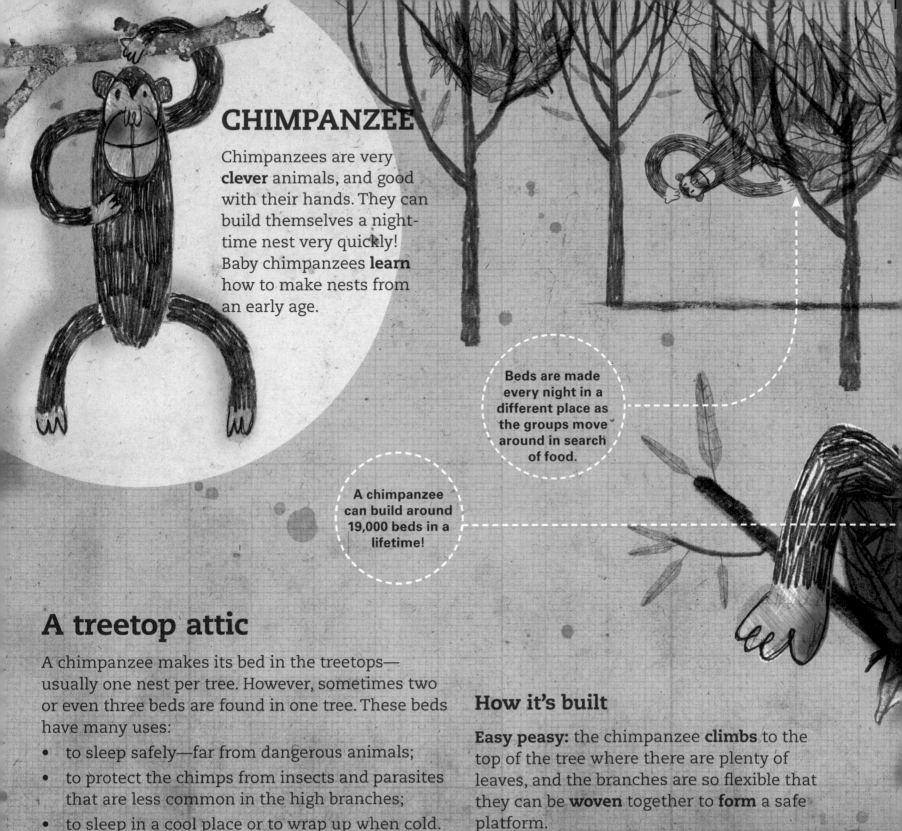

CHIMPANZEE

Chimpanzees are very **clever** animals, and good with their hands. They can build themselves a night-time nest very quickly! Baby chimpanzees **learn** how to make nests from an early age.

Beds are made every night in a different place as the groups move around in search of food.

A chimpanzee can build around 19,000 beds in a lifetime!

A treetop attic

A chimpanzee makes its bed in the treetops—usually one nest per tree. However, sometimes two or even three beds are found in one tree. These beds have many uses:

- to sleep safely—far from dangerous animals;
- to protect the chimps from insects and parasites that are less common in the high branches;
- to sleep in a cool place or to wrap up when cold.

How it's built

Easy peasy: the chimpanzee **climbs** to the top of the tree where there are plenty of leaves, and the branches are so flexible that they can be **woven** together to **form** a safe platform.

Chimpanzee
Characteristics:

Weight: females from 55 to 110 pounds, males from 75 to 155 pounds.

Height: 3 to 5½ feet.

Habitat: tropical forests and wet savannahs of central and western Africa.

Behavior: live in groups of 20 to 150 members.

Feeding: mainly vegetarian diet.

Enemies: big cats and hyenas.

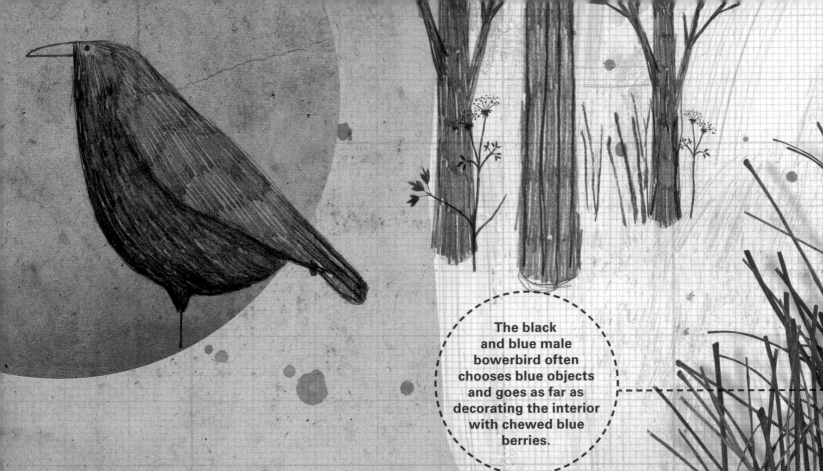

The black and blue male bowerbird often chooses blue objects and goes as far as decorating the interior with chewed blue berries.

SATIN BOWERBIRD

This medium-sized **bird** is a true architect and interior decorator. The male **builds** gazebo-like structures just to **charm** and impress the female. The birds use different colors, depending on the species. Interestingly, the males with the least colorful feathers are the ones that build the most **striking** constructions.

The lover's gazebo

The male builds a beautiful gazebo to impress the female and makes a real effort to decorate it with beautiful objects.

How it's built

Carefully: the male starts by **gathering** similar-sized branches to build the walls in a wing shape. He also **creates** a passage for the female to go through.

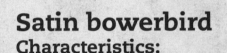

With tricks: then he looks for all sort of objects (stones, shells, seeds, and human objects) to create an optical illusion to impress the female. The trick involves arranging objects in a triangle form, with the small ones closer to the exit than the bigger ones. This way, from the passage, they all look the same size. The bowerbird never stops embellishing the gazebo to make it more attractive than those of other males.

Satin bowerbird
Characteristics:

Weight: around 7 ounces.

Length: males from 11 to 13 inches.

Wingspan: 13 to 15 inches for males.

Habitat: forests and mangrove swamps in Australia and New Guinea.

Behavior: solitary birds even during breeding. They only meet for a short time after a long and complicated ritual. They are excellent sound imitators.

Feeding: seeds and insects.

Enemies: snakes and other birds.

The hummingbird's long beak is perfectly adapted to the flowers from which it feeds.

HUMMINGBIRD

The hummingbirds include the smallest species of all the birds. They are also the only birds capable of flying in all directions: upward, downward, forward, and backward; even upside down! As they hover, they flap their wings around 75 times per second. They obtain their food while hovering.

A tiny apartment

The female builds a small nest:
- to incubate two eggs—no more, no less;
- to rear and protect her chicks.

How it's built

A good spot: the female **chooses** a branch hidden by dense foliage where she hangs or places the nest. Sometimes she builds the nest under a leaf to shelter it from the rain.

Her large beak is used to **weave** the nest, linking plant fibers together with very fine and flexible twigs. She uses spider web silk to **tie** all the materials together and attach the nest to the branch. Then she makes a comfy mattress with soft materials like feathers and animal fur.

Moss, lichen, dried leaves, and bark are used on the outside to cleverly **camouflage** the nest.